I

AM

CREATIVE!

And
it all starts
from
a
dot

I

AM

CREATIVE!

And
it all starts
from
a
dot

Tess Villegas-Rumley

© ARTESS, INC.
77-6411 Leilani St.
Kailua-Kona, HI 96740

Preface

Our creativity is just within our reach. This magical force dwells and is always present within each one of us: children, young and adult. It is fully alive and active in all of us.

This book will guide you in a very simple, easy and fun way how you can encounter and connect with your own creative self. It only starts from a simple dot...

As you read this book, tap it in, let the child in you flow and play with your creativity. Be inspired... it is a lot of fun!

Tess Villegas-Rumley

My overflowing gratitude...

The creation of this book could have never come to life without those magical moments of encounter and connection with the following gift of persons:

Sab, the 10-year old daughter of my best friend who at the age of five I already noticed the creative prowess flowing out from within her... so, every time I talk to her over the phone (they now live in Seattle) we talk a lot about creativity. It was last year in September 2011, as I told her to continue honing her gifts that with so much excitement she answered me: "yes, Granny, and it all starts from a dot!" Those words struck me so magically that all of a sudden ideas about the connection of the dot to creativity were just overflowing... Sab, thank you so much for the pure wisdom and for unlocking the magic dot for me!

Martin, my nephew from the Philippines whom surprisingly called me up while I was putting the book together...as I was sharing with him the last pages, easily and effortlessly, he uttered: "In fact, when God created us, He placed a dot in our mother's womb." Mart, thank you for completing the book and for making it whole! Our special connection goes beyond distance, space and time.

Gille, "the man who paints with his nose" whom one day, in August, last year showed up in his wheelchair in front of our gallery... my husband and I thought he has ALS disease only to learn from him that he was born with Cerebral Palsy. When I asked him what inspires him to paint, even though we could hardly understand him when he talks, the word came out so clearly: "SOUL!" Gille, you are a living testimony of a human being who is almost stripped of all the physical capabilities, but not your creativity! Thank you so much for showing me that the creative part of me is the expression of my soul!

Kira, extremely creative and our friend, although we rarely see each other , our connection is so natural, so human and yet truly divine, and so much fun! Thank you for helping me edit the book, darling!

Bonnie and Cal, my very first wood art patrons…Thank you for affirming me all the time that "you don't only like the piece that you bought, but that, you love it!" It's amazing how our encounter through my wood art has evolved into a beautiful and special bond!

Sandra, my sister and my first art patron. Thank you for making me aware that I am creative!

Steve and Anna of Kona Business Center, thank you for the computer work collaboration! You're the best!

And to all those encounters whom we have shared the language of creativity, thank you for enriching my creative journey!

This book is dedicated to:

Nanay, (my mother) for being the instrument of the magic dot for my creation...

Tatay (my father), Daibing (my sister), Lalal (my special auntie), and Mother Margaret, (my mother-in-law) for being my angels in heaven and for being with me in spirit all the time...

Preston, (my stepson) and my younger brother, Vinson for empowering my heart to continually believe that no matter what happens to our physical being, our creative self will never give up on us...

John and Beb, (my brothers) for always being available when I need their help and support...

Zoring, (our extended younger sister and my best friend) for being my super angel on this planet...

Ronnie, (my husband) for constantly inspiring me to connect to my creativity and for loving the all of me... I love you, Sweetheart!

And to Ryhya, Kikay, Mamo, Shokoy, Kristian, Trish, Kean, Dadang, Ssah, Will and all the children in the world whose creativity is so transparent, this book is especially dedicated...

To parents, grandparents and adults who think they are not creative or may have forgotten their creativity, this book is for you…

I

am

creative!

And

it all starts

from

a

simple

dot

●

I

let

it

flow...

and

let

it

flow...

Just

by

the

magic

of

my dots...

the

magnificence

of my creation

unfolds!

As I let my magic dots

flow naturally,

its connectedness

to one another,

either big or small

creates a

shape...

It looks

like a

circle!

Let me play

some more

using

my magic dots...

That's

the word: PLAY!

Yes,

I'm playing

with

my creativity...

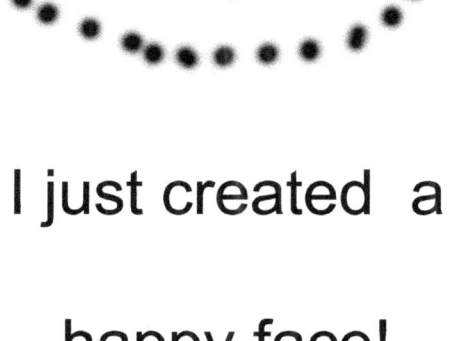

I just created a

happy face!

Playing

with my magic dots

is exciting!

It loosens me up,

brightens my day,

and brings so much joy

to my heart!

And

besides,

it's

very

empowering!

Hmm...

let

me

explore

more...

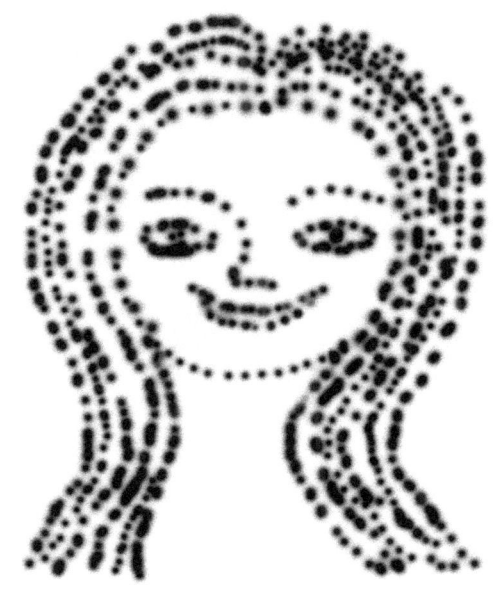

Aha, I just added more magic dots which gave my happy face her own beautiful, long hair!

This is cool!

More and more

I discover that I can

create all kinds

of shapes other than

lines and circles

from my magic dots...

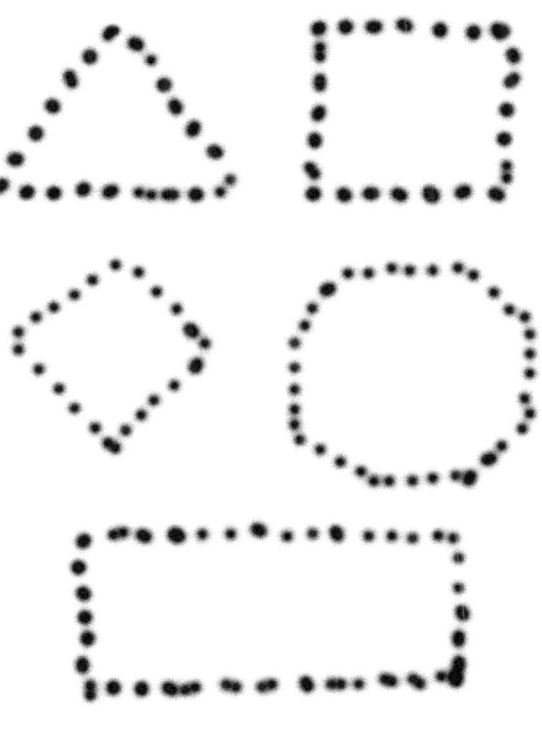

They don't have

to be perfect...

Guess what?

As I look around

my surroundings,

there is so much

I can create

using

my magic dots...

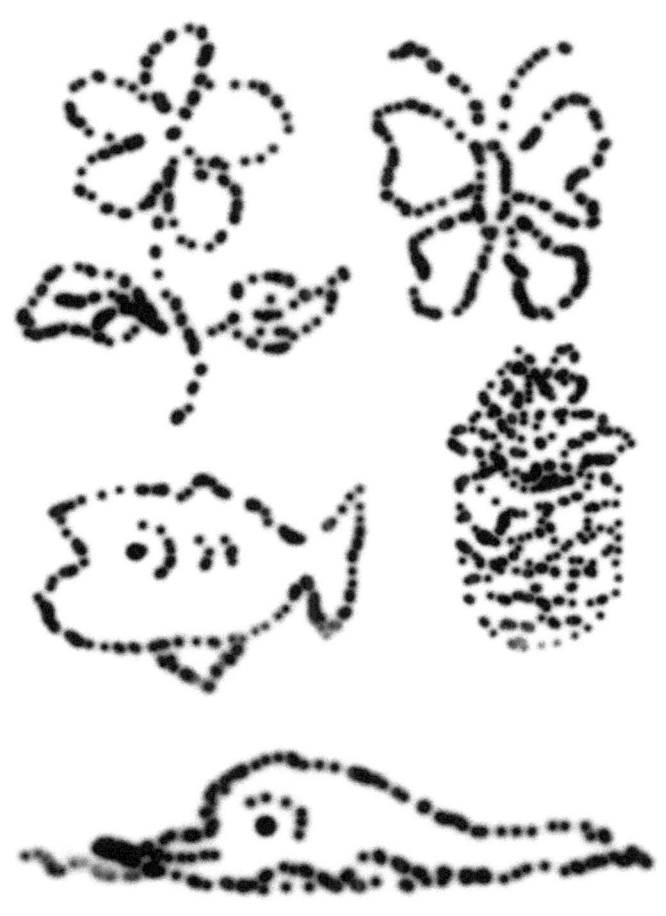

This is fun!

One thing

I've discovered

in the process...

as

I expand

my magic dots,

my imagination

expands

as well.

Also, I realized

that

SPACE

is extremely important

to

my creation.

It is the venue

or the environment

that allows me

to express

my creativity and

put it

to life...

and

at the same time

for my creation

to grow

and

shine!

Let

me

continue

my

creation...

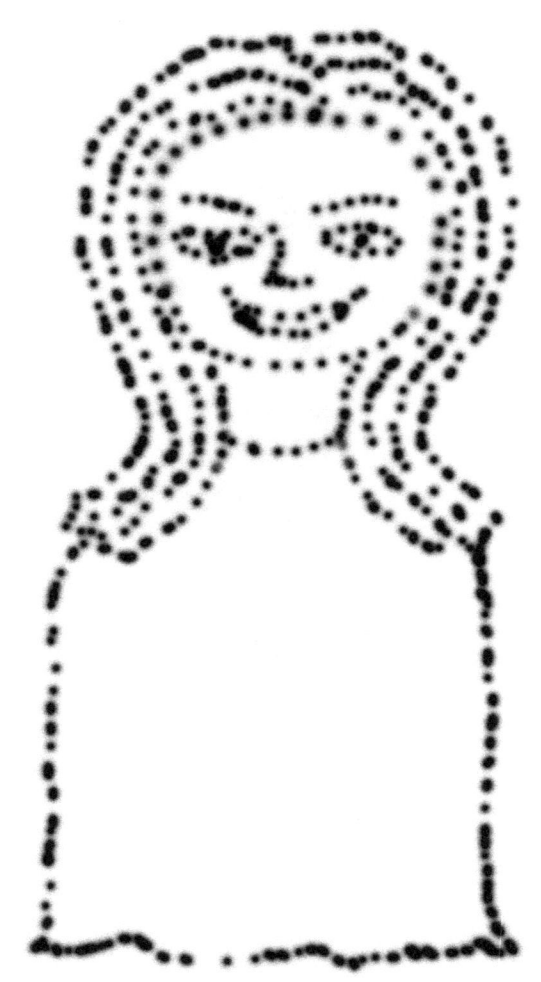

I created a simple dress!

It's

fascinating

that

my

magic dot

is

evolving!

I'd like

to put more

magic dots

on the dress...

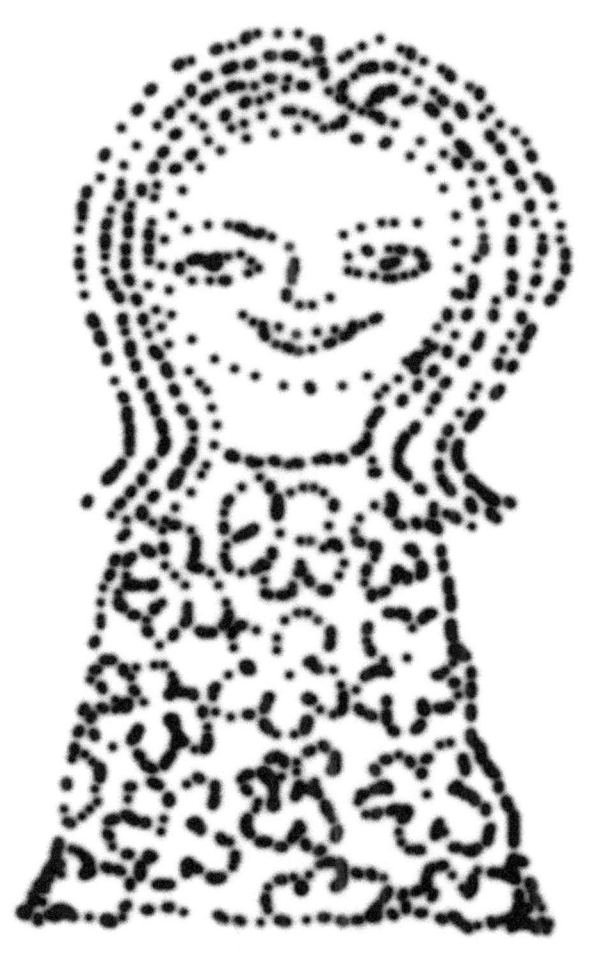

Flowers...

It looks pretty good!

Wow!

I'm enjoying

and

loving

this creative

exploration!

I observe that as

I create my magic dots

it's not just

about trusting myself

and

being courageous...

It's more

about allowing

and

letting creativity

within me

to come out and

flow naturally...

easily

and

effortlessly...

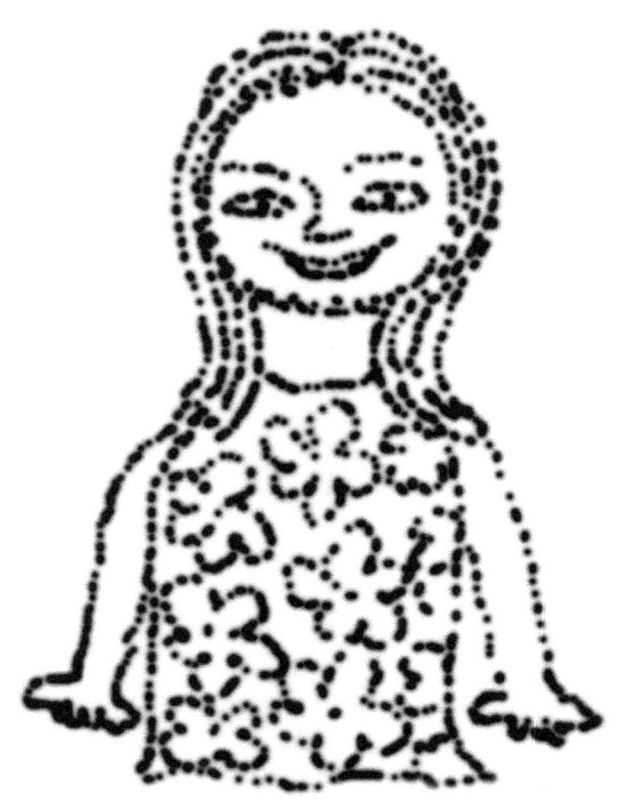

Now, I've got two arms
and "hang loose" signs
in my hands!

These magic dots

are amazing!

They are

so abundant

and limitless...

and so,

is

my

creativity!

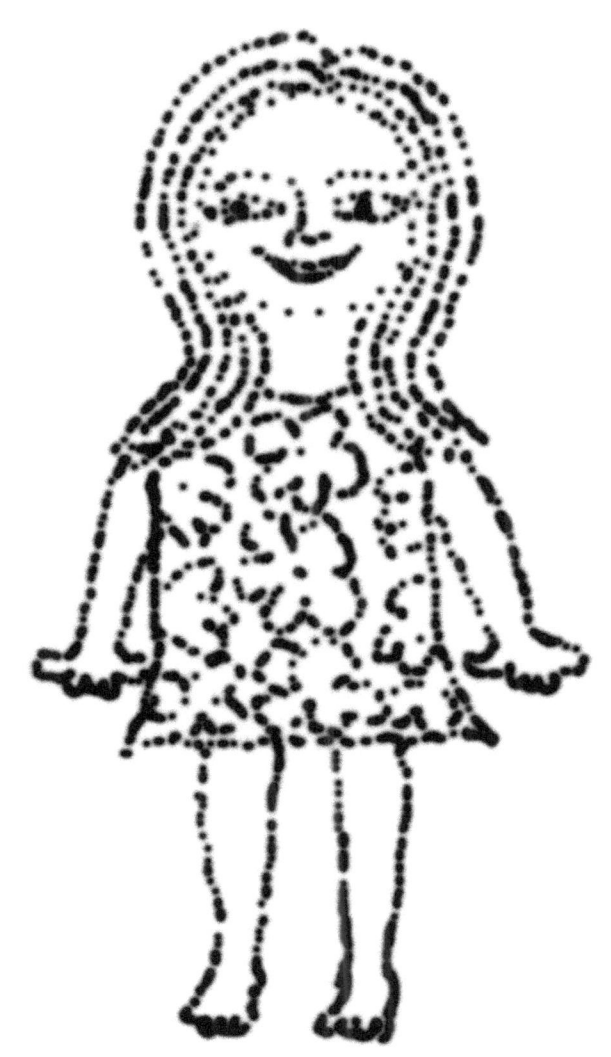

Look at that! I created legs
and feet to complete me!

Oh,

wait

a minute...

I won't feel complete
without "FLIP-FLOPS" on my feet!

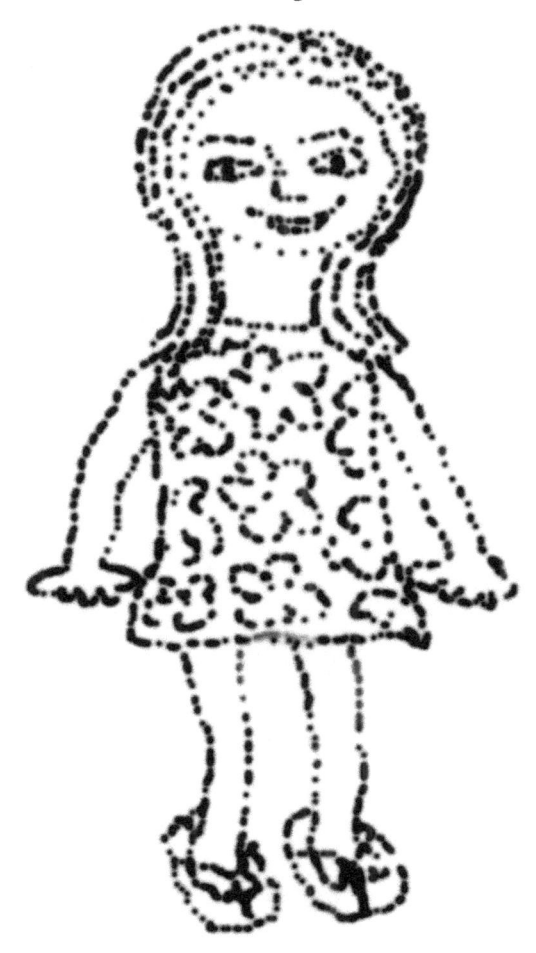

Right before my eyes
I witness the beauty and
wonder of my creation!

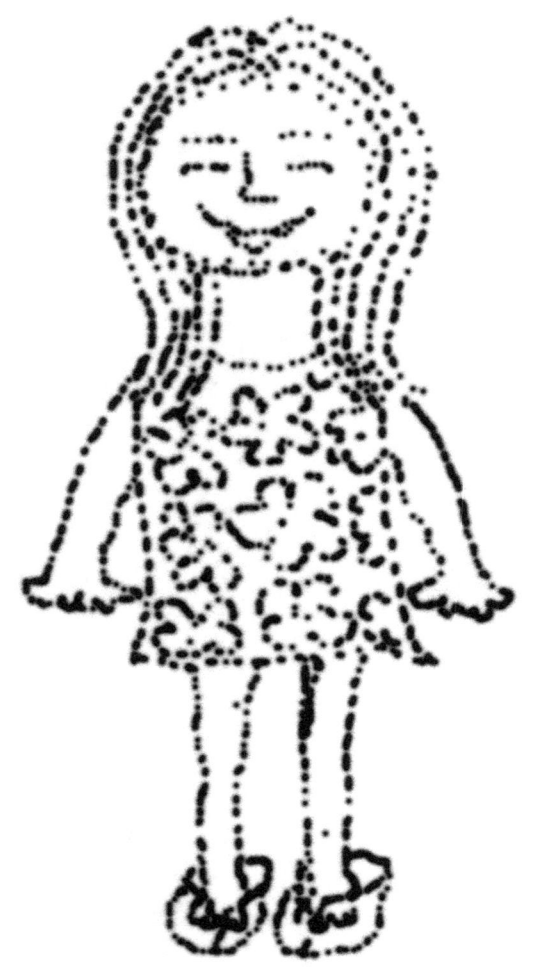

By allowing

the flow

of my creativity,

I

have

created

myself.

Every

creation

has its own

LIFE FORCE

within...

In fact,

when

God

created

me...

He

placed a

dot

in my

mother's womb...

And

I grew

and

grew

from that

magic dot...

to become

the

creative

and

beautiful person

that I am!

I

am

radiating creativity!

And I can

feel it

flowing through

me!

Unleash

your creative prowess

and

create your

own

magic dots...

it

won't

cost

you

anything...

A piece

of scrap wood

or paper,

a pencil

or your

writing pen...

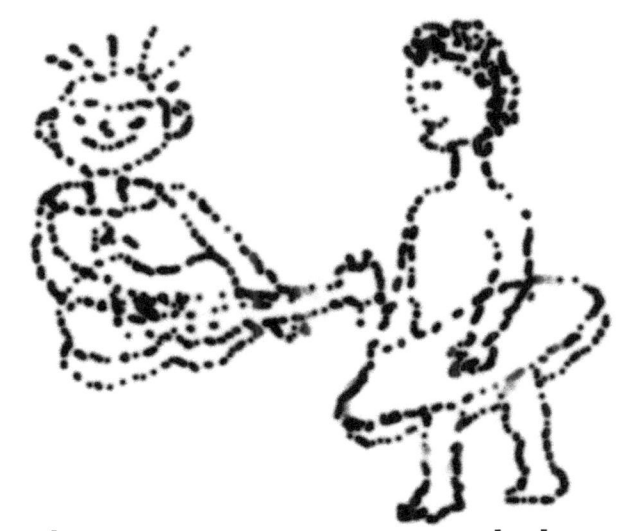

or how ever you wish

to express

your

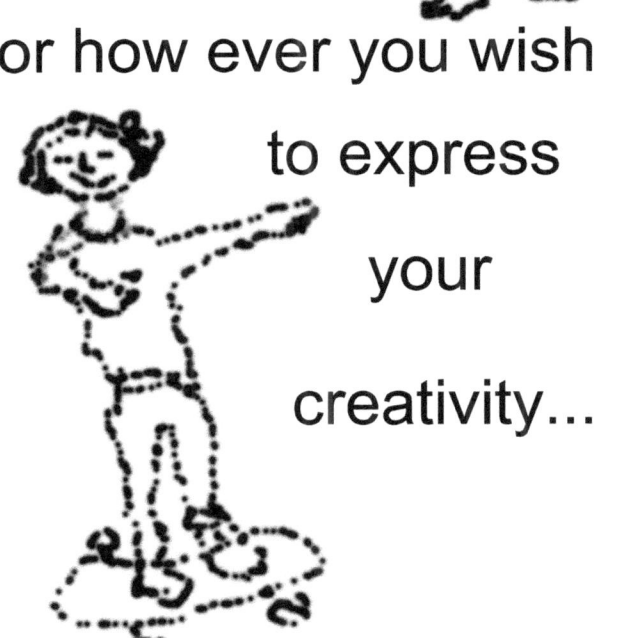

creativity...

Welcome

and

embrace

your

creative

self!

Have

fun

playing

with your

imagination...

Tap it in

and

connect with it!

here and now...

This

is

the

moment!

DO

IT

NOW!

WE

ARE

ALL

CREATIVE!

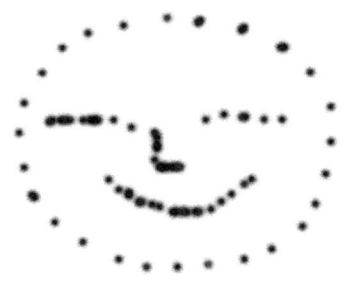

My deepest appreciation to:

Karen Kahmann for opening the way to limitless possibilities…

Marc Allen for the generosity in sharing his story of affirmations to humanity… Sir, it does really work! It's amazing how the universe provided me all the encounters and connections so that this book will be put to life!!!

I AM CREATIVE! And I let it flow…

Book Two Series to follow…

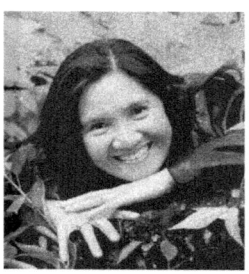

About the Author

Tess Villegas-Rumley is a graduate of Bachelor of Arts major in English Literature at the University of St. La Salle, Philippines. At the age of six, she knew there's that magic and wonder flowing out from within her, however, it was only when she reached thirty that she started to truly connect and playfully explore her creativity.

In 2005, she moved to Hawaii and got married. Being on the Big Island afforded her tremendous opportunities to evolve and further expand her creativity. Besides visual arts and photography, she creates unique and one of a kind pieces of wood art using the exotic local wood of Hawaii. She is also a custom picture framer and a printmaker.

With simplicity and humility, her gratitude is overflowing in the awareness and acknowledgment that our Creator who endowed her with abundant creativity is the Source of it all!

Tess and her husband own an art gallery, custom framing and archival giclee printing at Kailua- Kona, Hawaii inside the Courtyard by Marriott King Kamehameha's Kona Beach Hotel.

For more information, visit the websites:

www.rumleyartandframe.net
www.konacoastgiclee.com
www.konaedibleartcafe.com